POST
HUMAN

POST
HUMAN

Nate Pritts

© A-Minor Press
http://aminorpress.com/

Cover art by Eryk Wenziak (www.erykwenziak.com)

Book layout by Walter Bjorkman

ISBN-13: 978-0692598788 (A-Minor Press)
ISBN-10: 0692598782

First Edition, A-Minor Press

Acknowledgements

Some sections of "Pattern Exhaustion" were published (as "Untitled," or dated fragments) in *apt, Forklift, Ohio, Gesture, Ghost Ocean, Ghost Town, InDigest, Similar: Peaks::* and *Trigger.* A long section, titled "December" was published by TENDE RLOIN and, later, in a limited edition pamphlet with drawings by Lizz Thabet. Thanks to those editors for early encouragement.

Pattern Exhaustion was published as a chapbook by Smoking Glue Gun Press, and deep thanks are due Taylor and Blake Lee for particular insight.

The Equalizer, Second Series, published an early version of "No Filter." Thanks to Michael Schiavo.

Throg Sludge published some sections of "Ship of Nails" as five individual poems. Thanks to Aaron Tieger.

Some sections of "Life Event" were published in *BOAAT* and *Powder Keg.*

Special thanks to the A-Minor team (Nicolette, Eryk and Walter) and to Jenny - for everything.

TABLE OF CONTENTS

PATTERN EXHAUSTION

I forget myself
but I remember the morning
radio news   the contradictory
forecast of high clouds & sun.
I wear my new jacket

the one I am still getting used to

        so I don't have to wear a sweater
& because I'm vain & hope
it makes me look difficult

& severe.   It erases
my soft neck. I use the plastic trigger
to open my car windows

when I drive from one place
to another   don't even feel
the wind I'm supposed to

but I know enough science
to react appropriately.

Between classes I spend
twenty minutes looking
at photographs online

      high resolution American hush
          felt most especially
when seeing the dynamic
moments stopped   the camera

singling out only one thing
      that happened to keep forever.

Outside the hectic street quiets
since there are no words to help us
navigate our feelings or dictate
which thing to look at next.

I forget how to be solid.

Sometimes I keep my eyes
on the clouds
     & fumble
    to fit my hand in my pocket.

I loaded down my jacket
with stones I picked up
in various states at certain times
     I wanted to remember

but knew I wouldn't.

I listen to a lot of music
     but when I know a song is

about to end
      I stop it early.

Yellow leaves
      tumble
    through the air

& I feel momentarily special
though really everything we see
is rare   & won't happen

again.

I whisper every bad thing
I've ever done in crowded places
so I can't hear myself.

      When lots of people talk at once
I feel absolved of needing
to make sense.

             I am convinced
I am still a good person.

I watch this one girl   gently
press the back of her hand
      to her forehead

& do the same thing.

I have to guess at the right words

to email a student to explain
that she's failing.
                    I run a Google search

to find the closest Ethiopian restaurant.
I want to shake off any sense of time
          & not feel so trapped.

The smell of rain makes me nostalgic
for a beach I visited every summer
          when I was younger.

The sand spread out in a crescent,
          the sun rising & setting

in a relentless & unbroken sequence.

I read one specific email
fifteen times to really feel it

let it become part of the texture
of my day.   Sharp red afternoon
caught in leaves
                    raucous evening wind

        the dark. The end
doesn't look or feel like the beginning.

I close my eyes
when they're worn out
                from being so open.

I can forget one specific evening
or four whole years   even your name
as easily as summer forgets

        the blue of July turning
quietly to August. Now it's October.

I lift my head from the pillow
& the whole room is startling
white.
   I can feel
air breaking around me.

I try to name every cloud
in a crowded sky.

I'll never know if I get them
right.
   I wish there was someone

to tell me the answer.

   Relentless grey stratus
   mostly filling the horizon,
a few cirrus wisps near
where the sun burned
a hazy gap.

I check my email
for a message from you

twenty-three times

during a typical workday.
I'm too surly

& depressed about everything
        about even my shirt.

This far into the season
                    I forget everything

I ever knew about
summer. I take different herbs

to repair my memory
                    but irregularly
which probably sabotages
the desired results. Without

even looking   I know cumulus
gathers into a crayon lump.

I see so many new people
I didn't even know existed.

I watch the lights from three planes
blink past my window
                before
I say even one word

                        out loud.

Absence is the experience
of loss   or of waiting.
The frame for the picture

is made of wood remnants
from the same house
            you see in the picture.

It came apart under
            the weight of its own
story.
                I sit still   unraveling.
I listen to the same song

five times in a row before
I decide to do something more
noble with my life. Then

the moment passes.
            I drink two cups of coffee
though

                it's after 7:00 pm.

I spend forty minutes
imagining what it would be like
to stand in the rain

but never consider going outside.
                    I write a note

to myself so I won't forget
certain key data.

My thinking takes place
in words on paper.

                    I can no longer
dream myself toward workable

                  solutions.

I use my receipt for a bookmark
so I can remember myself
                  & my desires
into the future.

Everything is bright.
                        The clouds
the leaves   the air saturated.

I feel better about myself
when there is a lot of mail.

I tend to jump around
                    or
move from task to task.
In this way

              dinner gets made
the clothes folded & put away.

I write out a few more sentences.

I can't think things into clear
shapes anymore.

                I am too distracted
to kiss you right.

                    I pretend
to concentrate so I don't have to

wave at my neighbors
who are all smiling & expectant
            & don't understand.

It's so hard to be brave

when there's so much we don't know.
I try to remember a dream

so I can type it out clearly.

My tired morning fingers
            hit the letters
in the wrong order.

The air is suffused with
            a white light.

It's never interesting when people
talk about their dreams. I change
my mood.

I can't feel fully good

about anything. So I take a walk

& turn right onto Franklin Street
follow it until it stops
          then walk back

under the overhanging trees.

They barely hold back the rain.

I think about two or three friends

I haven't seen lately.

I try to remember one significant detail

about each of them.

I like it

when I can almost see through
my hands.

I have learned that rain is easier
to deal with when it ruins you
completely.

I have a feeling & I don't know
what to call it.
                    It only lasts

as long as there is sun
to fill out the morning hours

& then everything about me
stabilizes.

                    I type the symptoms
into a search engine
            to see if anyone else has a name
for this concoction.

I wish
I could believe in something
            that I could understand

instead of needing all this faith
            in unquantifiable things.

I am often alone. Then
I tell hello to the same person
                    five times in one day.

I never know what to say next
            since I spend so much time
            narrating my life.

When I open my mouth

I don't know where to start.
I use Google Maps

to see the Charles River
          better since it was raining too hard

when I crossed it for real.

I had to
keep my eyes focused   trained

on the objective. I want to be perfect

held whole & forever
                    in one moment.

I zoom in close to see the water

click the plus sign & drag it around
to look from both sides of the bridge
on my screen

& then click the minus sign

to get a different perspective
on all the streets that run around it
                because I don't know where

I really am / where I've really been in my own actual past.
        I think about living in a different house
as a different person. I really am happiest

when imagining.

Think for five minutes
about whether repetition suggests emphasis
or mania.
     The leaves the leaves.

Syracuse / this season.

Everything a pattern that can be
discerned   or else
   everything a pattern

because we say so.
Make a silent deal
with yourself to do something
    only if

one specific other thing happens.

If that leaf falls right now I'll.   Now.

Starting now.

If that leaf falls right now.

  Elements that could be introduced.

  Elements that are happily forgotten.

  Finally everything forgotten.

I'm losing the structure inherent

in my own thought or I'm just lazy.

I listen to pop punk & eat a lemon bar.

More than almost anything else

I want to go to the mall tonight

& maybe buy something.

Another day with no clue how to feel

since there's no television in the room

to tell us what apparatus we need to make us

thoroughly real to ourselves.

Wait   the song will change

even if I don't do anything.

The computer says it's thirty-nine

degrees outside which sounds right.

Music in my brain disintegrates / just metal

& crayon emotion

holding one long syllable to show they mean it

while I do so many things with my eyes

I don't even understand.   I am trying to become more

empathetic so I am thinking hard about how to feel

          reading a lot of books & avoiding messy people

in order to focus my sensibility & give it all shape   .

The postman brings new boxes almost everyday

& I make coffee in the afternoons when it is quiet

when it should be snowing.

I get distracted & turn the page

early to find where the endnotes are going to point me

because my conscience is already formed

which means none of this matters   reaction & action

the stimuli presented to me & my lack of definitive response.

I give over enough time to my uneasy worry   abstract

moral principles & the right response

                                        which eludes me.

I lay on the couch for fifteen minutes

& feel guilty about it   because nothing

is accomplished & I don't feel better.

I am losing all cognitive & temporal control

of this day / I can't even get my voice back

from the radio playing the same songs

convincing me of what to love.

I only hear myself in simple time   simple

words together   smooth & so hard to

discern.

                    People can be trained to think of you

as a happy & sociable person even if the evidence

suggests otherwise

                              is something I tell a co-worker

to explain why I will not go to the holiday party.

I do go to the holiday party but I don't stay long.

I will dismantle the center of the world

& write about love because it's all that makes sense

when there are all these pieces / I try hard

to say something new & sometimes I do

but mostly I settle for saying the same thing

in a different way.   The facts aren't in my favor.

I do two loads of laundry / call it work

& feel fulfilled so I make lunch then worry

about how I'll manage to do anything lasting.

I spend a few minutes daydreaming about

how I'll look in my new author photos

what face I will have   or what outfit

I yawn a lot these days / 37 years old / because of this

partial continuous attention which gets me nowhere.

I can say that I am fully aware of everything

that is happening around me but can't feel

connected to any of it   trading a hard long look

for a glance that takes it all in but without depth.

I buy new pencils & a pad that looks professional

like it should be taken seriously & I watch myself

in the mirror while buttoning my shirt.

I look at thirty pages of recipes

because I want to choose the right one

to use up the box of root vegetables

sitting in my kitchen. It snows hard

for an hour & then melts fast.

Those heavy clusters of snow so beautiful

in the air & then so gone. I get disappointed

when I can't find what I'm looking for

in my shallow dresser drawer

or the boxes in the mud room.

I think of the book I'm reading

about a barbarian who is trying to save

some wizards from being assassinated.

I know a lot of facts   a lot of people too

but it all feels like accidental knowledge.

I find myself caring about what happens to the barbarian

even though the writing is pretty simple

& sort of bad.

    His only friend is his sword.

I keep hoping that something epic will happen

so I look diligently & lower my standards.

Recognizing & appreciating aspects of your life

is a sign of maturity but how can I pay attention

when so many things are happening

      when all I want is a new language.

Each word is a physical thing / I tell my students

I tell them   collect pictures that are beautiful

but then they can't explain why they pick what they pick.

We are living under a sun of motion that blasts us

with so much fast light we don't know what we see.

Sweetness   even the parking meters can be

horrible / silent in the snow & full of authority

reminding me that the images I hold

in my head were put there by the crush of want.

       In this, the season that forgot how to start.

The future is in the air.   I sing to the frozen plants

the whole world caught by surprise in all this cold.

People in their cars turn their faces to me

before they look back to the road. I keep singing

louder.   Sweetness   I would lay down

in the park & be happy if you would smile

in my direction.

I always try to keep three or four lines of poetry

in my head &   anyway   my brain is so full

of other noise. I open the car window

because it is snowing   12 degrees

I put them all down & keep driving & try

to think of something I was thinking about yesterday

        or I try to recapture a feeling I was having

& get nervous because it always seems as if

my life plays & gets lost.

The war is elsewhere   but everywhere

        can be a battlefield.

I rest my forehead on the window

for a minute too long & draw some stares.

I used to save all my drafts in a box

now I forget everything quickly

& listen to the rain / teach me more about

how to be better.

      I prefer to imagine

all the possibilities instead of committing to just one

so I end up having tremendous potential impact

which is enough for me.

I spend fifteen minutes at the drycleaners

explaining what I thought were very simple directions

& now I feel like everything about my world is going

to be different.   I hate to think I'll never see you

wear that dress again.

NO FILTER

I step out of the house
The taste of morning coffee
      still fresh on my tongue

I keep my head down
      ride my bike through the streets of this town
Because I don't want to see
      don't want to see what's to come
Do I think what I think
Because of somebody else
Or do I really believe it myself?

Graffiti
On the side of the bridge says ATTACK

ATTACK / ATTACK / ATTACK

Every person that I ever loved
Is just a trace on the screen today
Just a ghost in my soul
So I need to know
      do I feel what I feel
When the machine tells me to?

When can I believe in myself?

Help me believe in myself

Various birds
whisper their songs
muted
on the afternoon breeze

which carries further—
both the music &
its origin—
than any defined span
of simple air.

For example
there are sounds I heard
years ago
when I was a different person

made of other constituent elements
& subject
        to a dizzying array
        of requirements that have since been abandoned.

But you can never undo
an instance of attention.
You can't ever be free.

The heart is forever inexperienced. - Thoreau

I take a few fragments
from every landscape
& build a colossal patch-
work lacking context
which I walk away from
every night   into the night
over the purple ground
of perpetual evening
in which everything exists eternally
lost.

I imagine a picture of myself
on an arctic cliff
dressed for the end of the world
though you can't see me or my costume
because landscape dominates
the image,
not the single small mark I make—
joyous at last!—
separated from the heft of a life
that was like the drag
of wet clothes when you step
from the water.
Some days I fear I can't leave

my computer which is where
everything happens. But then I look
down at the stilled canal waters
& my eyes see new things.
My eyes are always seeing new things.
I miss when you could really lose

someone forever, like how music
erupts in my soul when I remember
anything: a whole person
sometimes or just to perceive
the time & motion of my own life
instead of this daily flood
of ephemera, this electronic life.

Dark mornings
abound   crowd the season.
You can't distinguish
the noise of wind
        the rilled air against leaves
from within the sinister engines
        of the rain.
I am recording
the final experiences of a human
on this planet   entangled
with nature.

My dream of brushing the grey from my hair
My dream of wandering lost
        in my own body
        in the skeleton of a house
        I should know a place
     familiar to me

like any memory
like talks we had   in which we planned
for some future exigency   a picnic at the sand bar

where the land doesn't gradually transition
to the water but instead just meets it   crumbling

everything sure & steady simply dissolving
     all of it just one more state of matter

things moving & changing
beyond our ability to touch them   to shape them
to be anything to each other

As long as I live in this head
baffled by its own intentions & decisions
I contend with this mistaken space
hard & blank
at the center of my spirit.
Better to walk out in the mornings
uncertain & glad
without trying to predict everything
with my own blunt instrumentation.
Everywhere I go, I damage the world
by trying to guess at it.

At my desk I move
        a few papers around
use a pen to weight down the scraps

because there's a wind coming through the house
washing over me like starlight in an open field

maybe Vermont   maybe
one of those nights between us
which I remember now like a passage

in a book   just words
meant to signify all the magic in a moment
        all the wisdom
        that terrible ephemeral construct

which is all we know
both of ourselves   & all these things that have happened

I don't even try to remember
I don't type lines

as the low murmur of the world
arranges the light by which we see
tricks us into believing a path away from
something might also be a way back

Great Blue Heron on the rocks
Near the edge of the water & I

Don't want to get too close
He's not a figure for something
        he doesn't have to carry my soul

All the sadness I keep packed inside

Then I get too close
        startle him into flight

I pretend for a minute that he's the last one left
What'll we do when he's the last one left?

What if I'm the last one left?

White light of the sun

All over the old wood of the porch

The leaves of the trees all around
Dumb green hands

Can't hold it back
        so it spills & it spills
A flood with one divine mission
        to bury everything here
   under mountains of tide

I try to imagine there's nothing moving
No one left
I can taste the trill of the insects
        on the back of my tongue

So sharp a song   so lonely
I pull it all in
        nothing left but me

Then I close my eyes & feel
Myself fall apart   gladly

Here I am at the table, these chairs,
all painted fresh to look worn.
They blend in with this present age
of getting whatever you want
even when you have no idea what that is.

We generate more waste.

The days will eat you alive if you let them.

SHIP OF NAILS

Inner wisdom activates you
Awakens you to yourself
The benevolence of the market god
The quiescence of morning as it unfolds
Watercolor sky above
So soft   So pretentious
          My thoughts

Things to be seen   seen clearly
Behind windows he points
With pixels on the screen he points
A gathering of heroes
A pile of nonsense the sound
The din the crash the utterance
Meander of day upon day or
Crush of day after day then

Extreme sharp grass blade covered in frost
Every action a buried profit motive
Every sunrise a momentary help
The hawk hanging in the air assaulted by birds
Something stolen that can't be returned
Hence people or even systems within people
What breaks down   What ends
What remains of what ends

Working toward objectives
The undone everywhere hidden inside tasks
Customized programs have been built
There's no way to share information
Is a dream a dream from the past
An environment is created   Simply is
Once begun   Neverending
Once thought   Only action remains
Fulfillment of those things we imagine for ourselves
We have predictable durability
We know the end to our story is part of our story

Using standard protocol we exchange
Share information with other mechanism
Accessing records
Accessing legacy applications
History is not sustainable
Now we seek the present moment in the present moment
Devoid of context we can't live
Gathering data during the data gathering period
We close the doors against the cold

There are two primary reasons for collecting
Everything aggregated through anonymised procedures
Every set unreachable
Sunflowers turn their faces to the wall
I have significant concerns about reliability
Raw processes   Raw data
Special rules of subjective documents
And we know that anything outside the target area is thus
Outside the target area is a blizzard obliterating
Corn snow heavy & damp on the ground

Once I was a unit building itself
Interacting with the environment
Taking things into myself
Now I process the process
We learn that deer are attracted by bright colors
We learn that sunflowers survive when they hide
Items held in my hands just held
We align facts with our need & refuse to verify
Something cannot be recalled

Deactivated weapons are still weapons
Input the code
Each occasion asks you to input the code
Or else come into contact with a new reason
This system may be impaired
Investigation is complete
Inactive for months there is an automatic process
I need something to keep my hands busy
A reminder of something to hang from the rearview

I am having trouble using this product
There's more time now   More time than ever
In times of famine   There is death
In times of plenty   There is death
Today I remember myself
The way I thought I would be yesterday
An alarm signals that something is happening
Everything else is up to you
We don't choose our deaths
There are so many favorable options

Him impenetrable
Mute behind living room windows
Autumn road is an image created
Red hillside tree the symbol
Ungrasped leaves   Hallways of yellow forever
Hindered by memory &
I am a closed system
With unwanted precognition
A broken system in need of repair
The theme of the day
That action leads to action
Unthought   A word underlined in red
Jagged red the underline
We are told thing that are real
Aren't real   Aren't things

Participates in life
Is memorable
Events are changing
Feelings are changing
Events suffer powerful feelings
A verbal artifact makes patterns
I mean   A linguistic artifact
Words on paper
I am suffering powerful feelings
In words on paper
I live viscerally   In thought
Live apart from all this own crude matter

LIFE EVENT

I don't have one story to tell

can't find myself by returni̇ ͜
to any unified narrative
          since I am always cycling / discovering more parts.
Coherence is not a value I believe in
          & has brought me nothing but pain.

You recognize some surface
          place your palm on it   follow it out
to the edges / the corners.
You've spent so many nights
          trying to learn a shape
you thought you could hold
              an object you thought you could give a name to.

So many miles of night & still
          no name for it   no understanding.

My poetry remembers & forgets
          this one self
              the way my life   has learned routines
only to leave them
to lose faith
              while my body empties of what it collects.

I don't have one story to tell

though I want to create something I can understand
          that puts pieces in even provisional place
temporary convenient demarcations
              even if just for today / right now
                              while I am lost.

Something that began somewhere.
Something that will end.

I want something that will end.

We buy a product
      & create ourselves

choose words   choose actions

       this activity / this being
          human that we are engaged in.

We build a new person on top of the old
constantly
     inexorably.

We are designed this way.
To inhabit one space   to fill it up
     to destroy it   to break it down
to leave it behind
       to leave it.

Every time I say goodbye to a friend
         to someone I love

I lose my way
                    & another life ends.

How can we manage all of these faces
         so many lives distracting us from moving forward
         from quiet focus.

We're split   into constituent parts

         it is no longer possible to unify.

The one that experiences the life
                              & the one that is quiet.

Coherence is not a value I believe in
         but I need it to exist   so I can deny it purely
              & with the risk of being wrong.

A heretic needs something to disavow.

I can't enjoy this morning
                deep rainy breaths
            buffered by a sky that curls around itself in layers of
color

because I'm not even here.
            All my energy is concentrated
on some point in the past
                        that drains this present attention.
I don't have one story to tell
            but I can't stop.

There are so many points of contact
            between consciousness & complex phenomenal
experience

& I am hundreds of other people

            each with responsibilities
cares / interrelations   all of which makes me
            human   all of which
I wish I could be rid of
                    cleansed so as to be only here
only now   pure
in this endless grey that breaks & breaks

            that brings light I am too distracted
to fully realize the beauty of.

The wind picks up   whole trees moving stiffly
        branches still naked so you can see

                they move wild but in proscriptive arcs.

Nothing like the shimmer of leaves in summer.

        The evenings long & light

                when any wind is welcome
any wind by any name
                                the sound of nature
        clattering against nature

                & this noise a kind of cloud
against what I imagine are the stark colors of my soul

        every memory   every happening

                a texture for the view   even the dark spots
an inexplicable context.

I have four books & some magazines stacked near my chair
         my coffee   some old letters
two years' worth
              because I am simply trying to remember.

I turn the light off   every light off   I try to breathe.

You can see the afternoon breeze passing through the open
window.
         The air is soft so soft   & so fading.

I drink my coffee & watch everything accelerate.

                There's one persistent clutch of green
         at the base of the ruined oak trunk.

I watch the horizon.

                I watch everything expire.

We've had it wrong. Life isn't accumulation.

Every day is a slow destruction.

      We trade every experience
         for grief at its passing.
Our years proceed   dismantling our loves / leaving
us.

The life we live isn't growing   but fleeing
      from usleaves us empty / pining
unable to appreciate the moments we'll miss tomorrow.

I want the stars to ruin us
                  our happy smiles.
Like bombs   made of time   transpiring
     to destroy everything all of us hold in our hearts.

      We think it won't change
    though it already has.

Everything gets lost   & only some things get found.
Somewhere in between is the only love we know.

I want the moon to be terrifying   a steady light
        Implacable   close

want the planet itself   the ground and the sky
to be seen for what it is.

            So cruel
so sad   so unpredictable.

Every movement whispers some other trace
       the cost.   I thought I heard it
          that heavy engine of regret
             roaring in my ears.
I couldn't ever be just here   but am a ghost
         a vanishing.
     Being here   am thus not   some place else.

At the grocery store I picked vegetables
       the ones that shined
         made my own choice
about what I'd need to make dinner

& this is such a small thing. It's almost not even worth
mentioning.
       But life is made of such fragile moments
      & we recognize them   we feel them happening

       we feel them slipping fast away.

       I don't have one story.
I concentrate on my happiness   try to let it burst
          & permeate
everything   the way flecks of hard orange light
           some mornings
      can make the day seem more real
& all our mute objects holy.

We can predict events based on previous patterns.
Such radiant actions throw off a haze of light
        & even the slow tumble of clouds
                follows the wind's trajectory

the future coming into us like a dream we remember
           or birds hanging throughout the trees.

It's how we know when we've committed
        to a path we'll regret   locked in
        that sensation forever
I have learned to regret everything

                              to feel
      even intentional steps   are steps away.

      It is a constant
           of my human condition.

I sitting here wondering
          how much longer the rain will hold
    off.

I work so hard to forget myself
      & now the trees are full of autumn.
This is the time of year   when I would rip myself apart
      if I thought it would do any good.

The cold seeps in   becomes more real than anything
real.

      Flowers drop their petals like rags
because they can't bear all this collection / recollection.
The lakes hiding among the hills

      hold their breath   hope no one comes knocking
& I am the man you do not want to see.

Morning by the pond & each bird shakes itself
awake   moves off violently

& I can't think.   It's too cold
      to forget my hands   that my whole body is
here
preventing me from falling away from myself.
      I don't have to tell one story.

You stretch   & feel yourself

     strain   dissolve

           & then hope to feel yourself fall apart

    to feel everything   separate

under its own weight

    its terrible human weight

      the weight of love

           too much of it

overwhelming & necessary

          & all this light

but when it doesn't happen
    you sit there still   inside the noise

of the present moment

     looking on in silence.

You get up from where you've been reading
          in small light   the sun too dim
                    to do anything except cast the sky
in a darker blue.
                    You pour more coffee

walk the whole pot upstairs
          to where she's sitting
by the window   typing herself into morning

          clarity   some unhurried & personal space
the kind that exists before emails & meetings.

Back downstairs you take pieces of rye bread
          palm sized   from close to the heel
toast them

& then sit at the table   spread knives
          of raspberry preserves over each
                    red & bright

the seeds suspended   blurry.
You eat fast   with purpose

or you don't
                              you linger
& waste the morning with these kinds of tasks.

But it's not you.   You don't do any of these things.

                    This is my life.

Clumps of grass look frantic.
                              The light reaches in

penetrates the cluster   charging it with green
                    with shadows.

I use up so many words
on normal tasks   all the response & business

& am emptied of any greater power
                    the energy baffled & torn from me.

My eyes can only see the simple shapes
that surround me
                              can relax & take comfort
in the consistent colors   that presence

but can't pull something new from the air

        can only breathe   & breathe again.

My own distractions   this intense pressurized crush
          has populated my thinking

& I embrace them all gladly   give myself over
to refusal
          of the happy serenity of involvement

which every time leaves me bankrupt & silent
leaves me mute & with nothing.

But it's true that every day
                         I write some lines of poetry

sometimes a patch of ten or
                    a whole stretch of fifty.
          Then when I read them later
I delete them

          or most of them

& end up with something loose
          which is another chance
to get it right.   So much is lost

which is something I can't do anything about.
I don't have just one story to tell.

Even these words only notate
some present state
          which is   fleeting
                    words immediately
blank to the living that aroused them.

My teeth ache because they are real
    & have lived a long time.

Each tree shreds the sky into pieces of sky.
I live so many different days

    over & over

with all this grief stuffed in my pockets
    & the sky still a mess   still torn.
You have to live through

    live through & forget

forget & then wander back.

I stand completely outside time
    happily lost
in my own backyard   a real place
that didn't exist yesterday

    because it was different
when my fear of the future was overwhelming

my experience of the present was deafening
in my ears
    the animal emptiness.

    I stand apart
from the experience of it all   the persistence of it
    so cold because of the actual weather

a feeling that I can feel   all the way through
without my mind distancing itself
with other kinds of loss   the way
a recording never sounds perfect

    especially when it sounds so close to perfect.

Each picture on any wall is never more than a reminder
of a single gone moment
                  among so many.

You step outside   in a rush of movement

      it is so hard to breathe the thin morning air

      like it isn't even there

& the heavy light covering the ground

making it hard to see the pathway   to the car

      down the driveway

      into the regularity of your life.

It's so bright   all this light

      all this joy   waiting

to accelerate   all the events

a simple blur of motion

      which makes no sense

a shattered path.

Then everything halts its inexorable movement forward.

You hesitate   you feel yourself

whittled down by time / worn smooth

      but unwilling to be diminished

even though there's nothing   so little   left to save.

I like to move around the kitchen
        quietly.
                    I pour my coffee
spike it   it's almost 3:00 in the afternoon.

When I write now I don't write about what I've done

but only about what I'm doing.   I don't remember

        so can only name up the impulses & compulsions that
occur

because I am so unhappy with many of the things I do.
I play a record loud because it reminds me
        of a certain time in my life / is a track

        I have retained dependable access to.

It's still sweet   still a tender type of time.
The sky turns from clear blue to solid white

        & then it hardens   as I watch it.
I take my mug outside feeling foolish.
        I don't have one story to tell.

            Earlier I saw a scattering of delicate color
                        just starting

slight petals in a tangle of woody bush
        & now I want to see it closer.

It's the kind of air that feels like rain
        & when it starts I'll go inside
to watch it.   I'll just watch it.

There are two birds, two sweet friends, who dwell on the self-same tree. The one eats the fruits thereof, and the other looks on in silence.

Svetasvatara Upanishad

Nate Pritts is the Director and Founding Editor of H_NGM_N (2001), an independent publishing house that started as a mimeograph 'zine.

He is the author of six previous books of poetry, most recently *Right Now More Than Ever* (2013). Publishers Weekly described his fifth book, *Sweet Nothing* (2011), as "both baroque and irreverent, banal and romantic, his poems […] arrive at a place of vulnerability and sincerity." *POETRY Magazine* called his *The Wonderfull Yeare* (2009), "rich, vivid, intimate, & somewhat troubled" while *The Rumpus* called *Big Bright Sun* (2010) "a textual record of mistakes made and insights gleaned…[in] a voice that knows its part in self-destruction."

Pritts is Associate Professor at Ashford University where he serves as Curriculum Lead and Administrative head of the Film program. He lives in the Finger Lakes region of NY state.

natepritts.com

Photograph by Edgar Praus

A-Minor Press
Current and Forthcoming Titles

Sam Rasnake, *Cinéma Vérité*

Mary Carroll-Hackett, *If We Could Know Our Bones*

Michael Keenan, *TRANSLATIONS ON WAKING IN AN ITALIAN CEMETERY*

Kate Litterer, *Ghosty Boo*

Nate Pritts, *Post Human*

In Memory of Walter Bjorkman (1948-2015)